Turtle Moon Press

pregnancy journal & coloring book

First Edition

Copyright 2016 by Lisa Greennut
All rights reserved.
ISBN-10: 0-9974589-0-9
ISBN-13: 978-0-9974589-0-9

For more coloring books and journals, and extra copies of the pages featured in this book, visit http://www.turtlemoonpress.com.

♡ Congratulations on your pregnancy! I wish you & your family all the best. ♡

my pregnancy

estimated due date:

♡ ideas for writing & coloring ♡

Start at the beginning. Or skip around. Leave pages unfinished, then return to them when the mood strikes. Honor your energy level - mental *and* physical. Do what feels relaxing, encouraging, and inspiring to you.

Don't worry about doing it "right".

What you'll need:

- a writing implement that feels comfortable in your hand

- coloring tools - I recommend colored pencils or fine tipped markers, though you can use anything you'd like.

- a few minutes to yourself

You may wish to test your tools out on the scrap page provided at the end of the book before using them. If a marker seems likely to show through, you may wish to use a piece of scrap paper underneath the page in progress.

Color in anything you'd like, any way you'd like. There are full mandalas, plus black and white borders waiting for your personal touch.

Choose the colors that speak to you. Try new combinations, or use your favorites again and again.

what's on your mind?

Pregnancy can be a time of great excitement, possibility, joy, and happiness.

Pregnancy can also be a time when we are bombarded with conflicting advice, dos and don'ts, intrusive questions, horror stories, and old wives' tales.

For you, it may be a time of worry, or simply of questioning. Will everything be OK? What will my life be like when the baby comes?

Who am I now?

use this book to hear your own voice and consult your own inner wisdom.

Congratulations from my heart to yours, from a fellow traveler along the journey into motherhood.

-Lisa

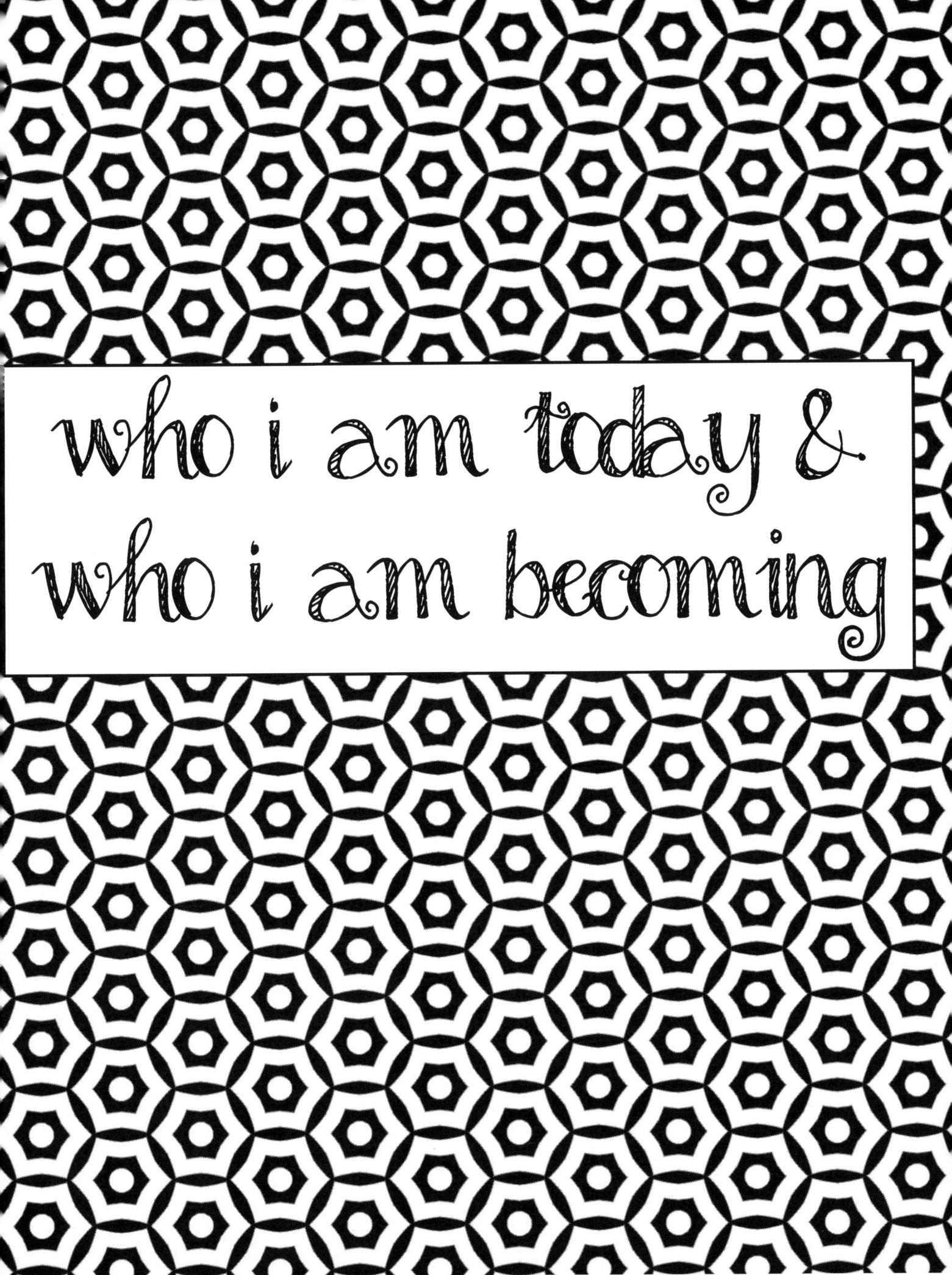

who i am today &
who i am becoming

what's important to know about you?
What do you love? What do you most enjoy?
What defines YOU?

what i want most in life is...

_____

_____

_____

_____

about our family

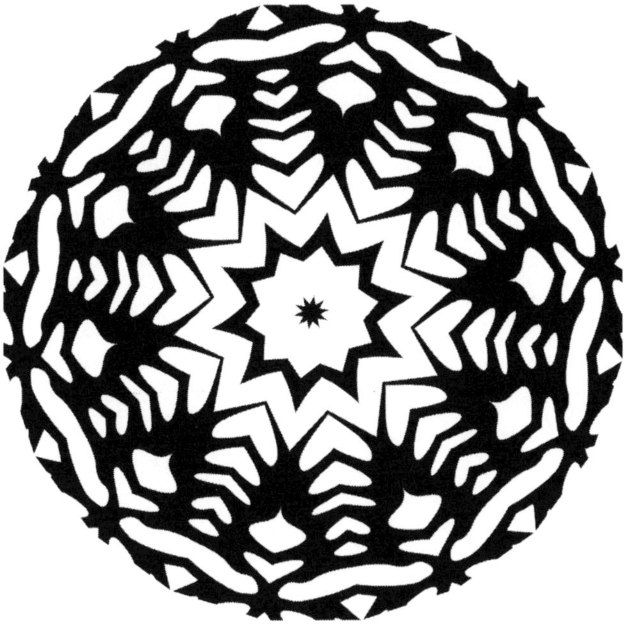

Write about the people, present in the world or here in spirit, who are here to love and support you and your new baby.

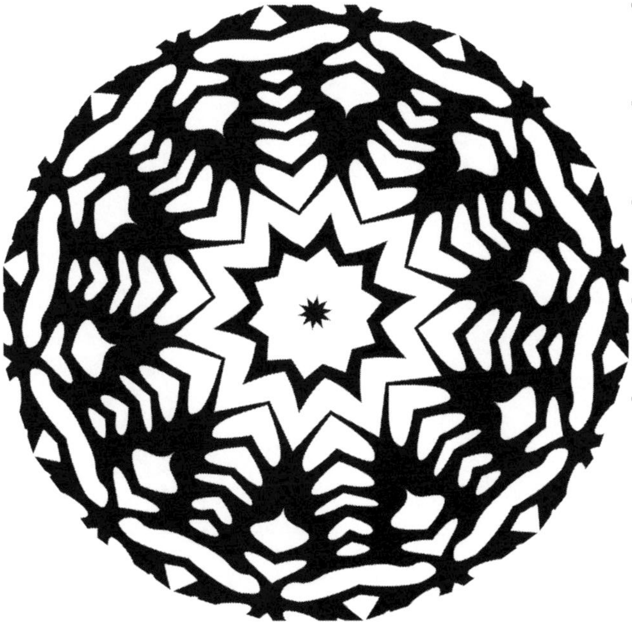

What family environment would
you like to create for your baby?
What will s/he have that you
didn't have?
What will you avoid?

family traditions

_____

_____

_____

_____

_____

_____

_____

_____

_____

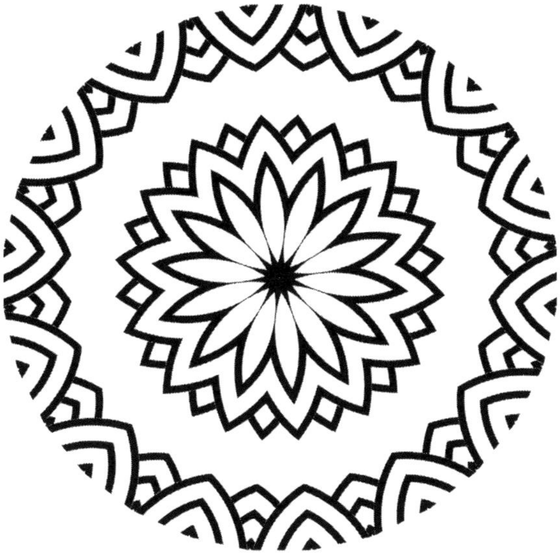

When did you know? How did you find out? Describe your feelings.

Was this pregnancy expected/planned? What are your feelings about how it happened?

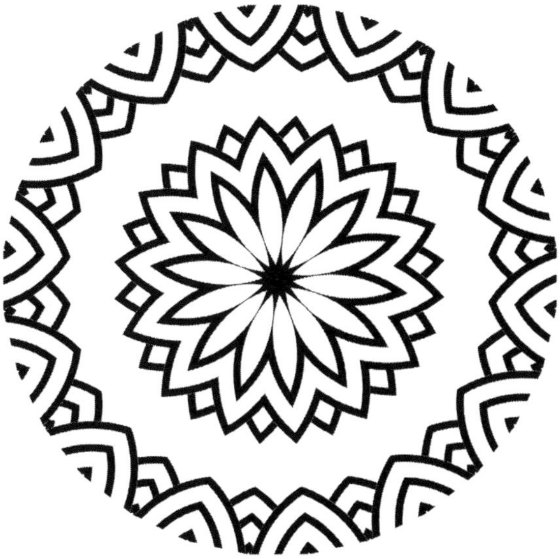

Who did you tell first? What was the reaction?

_____

_____

_____

Who else have you told?

_____

_____

_____

Who would you like to tell, but haven't yet? Why not?

_____

_____

_____

shopping list

_____

_____

_____

_____

_____

_____

_____

_____

_____

_____

things to do

_____

_____

_____

_____

_____

_____

_____

_____

_____

my baby's gender

Describe how you found out about your baby's gender (if you chose to). Will you tell others? If so, how? Why, or why aren't you sharing the gender before the birth?

_____

_____

_____

_____

_____

_____

_____

_____

names

What names are you considering for your baby? Write about the factors involved in your decision and which names you're leaning towards - or not!

_____

_____

_____

_____

_____

_____

_____

_____

how i pamper myself

_____

_____

_____

_____

_____

silly advice
and comments

_____

_____

_____

_____

_____

_____

_____

doctor visits

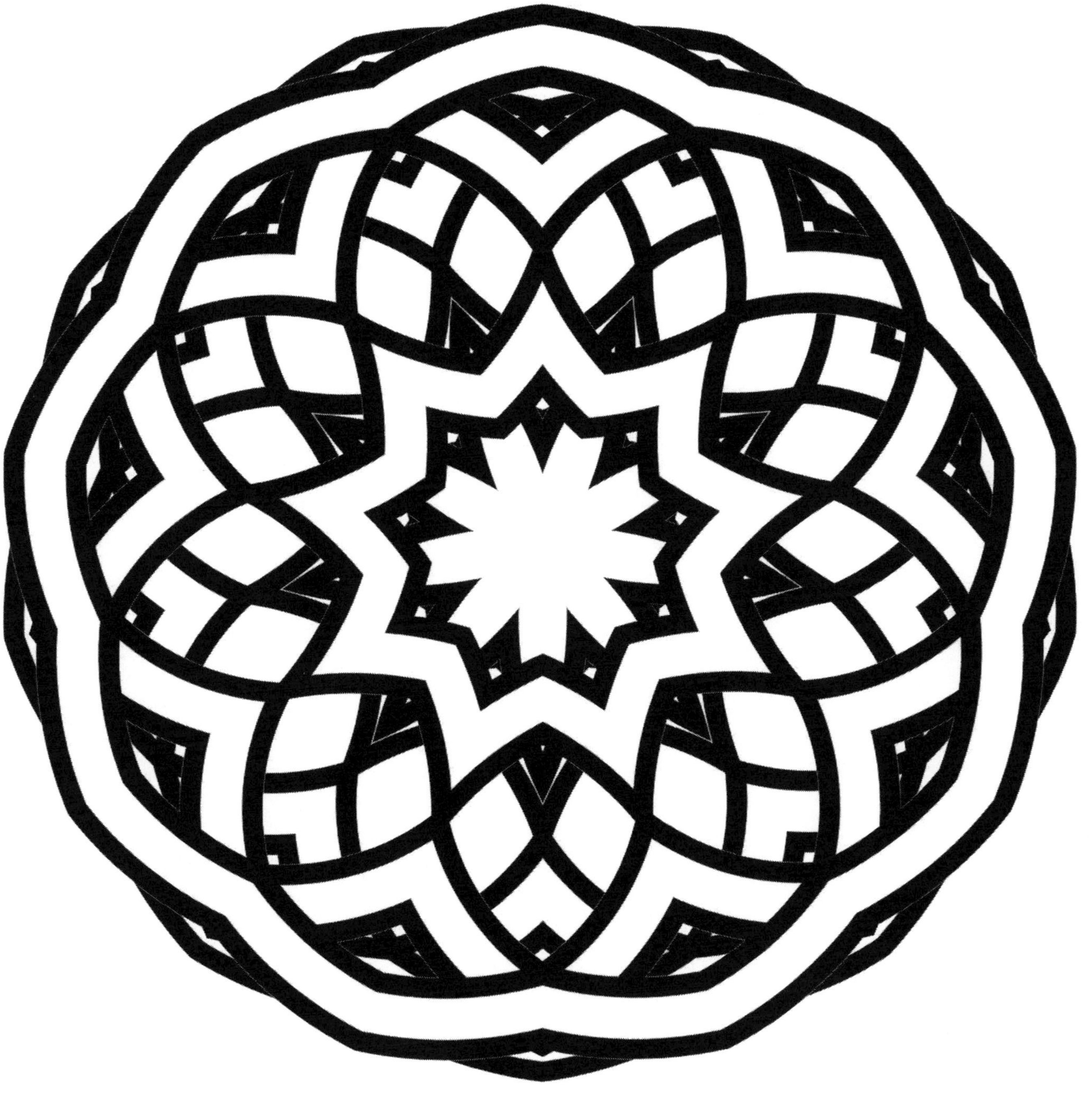

appointment tracker: ob visits

Date	Questions & Concerns	Answers/Follow Up

appointment tracker: ob visits

Date	Questions & Concerns	Answers/Follow Up

appointment tracker: ob visits

Date	Questions & Concerns	Answers/Follow Up

appointment tracker: specialists

Date	Questions & Concerns	Answers/Follow Up

choosing a pediatrician

Criteria: _____

_____

_____

_____

Offices to check out:

_____

_____

_____

_____

choosing a pediatrician - notes

_____

_____

_____

_____

choosing child care

Criteria: _____

_____

_____

_____

Places/People to check out:

_____

_____

_____

_____

choosing child care- notes

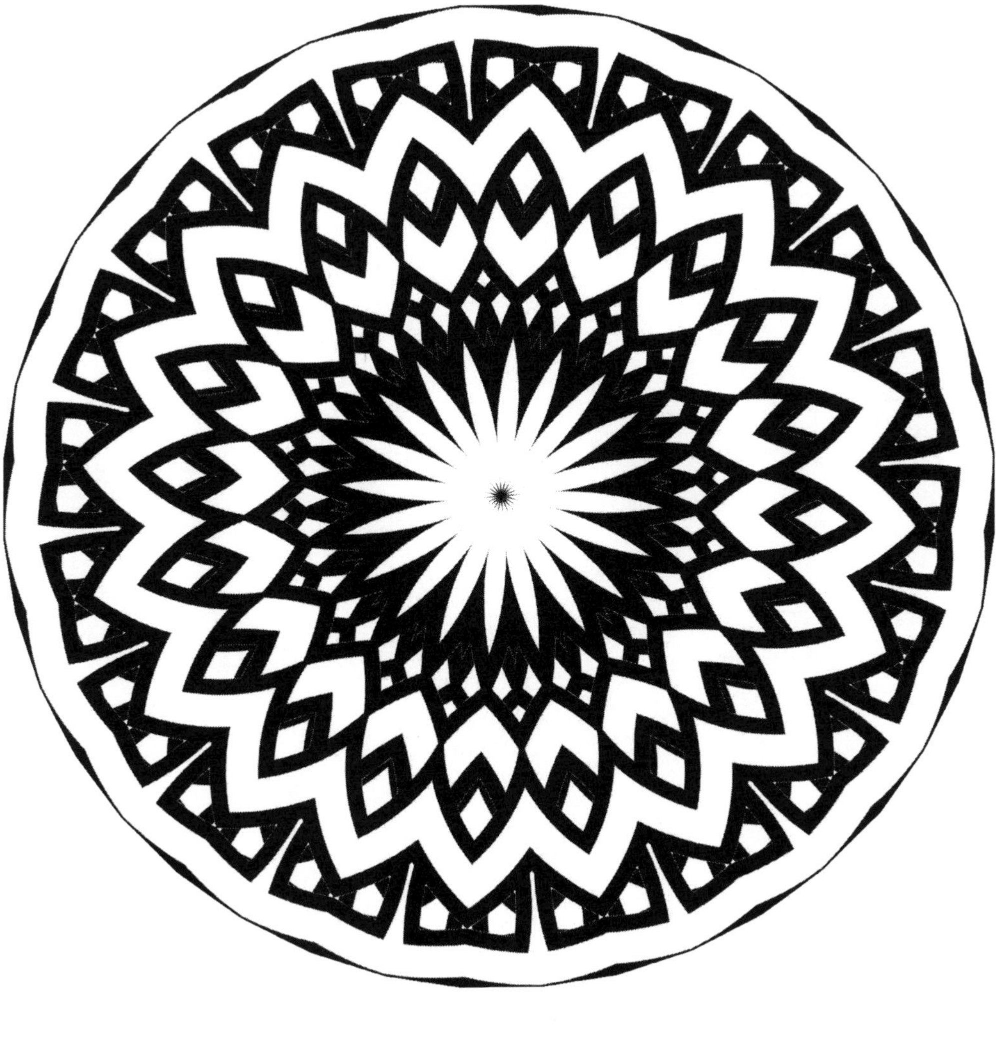

first trimester

weeks 1-13

a time of

beginnings

cross off the weeks as you go...

1 2 3 4 5

6 7 8 9

10 11 12 13

self care

Fill in the circles as you complete each action. Feel free to use the suggested actions, or write in your own.

take a bath
prenatal yoga
take a nap
drink water
talk to a friend

_____

_____

_____

_____

_____

◯◯◯◯◯◯◯
◯◯◯◯◯◯◯
◯◯◯◯◯◯◯
◯◯◯◯◯◯◯
◯◯◯◯◯◯◯
◯◯◯◯◯◯◯

◯◯◯◯◯◯◯

◯◯◯◯◯◯◯

◯◯◯◯◯◯◯

◯◯◯◯◯◯◯

monthly health tracker

Use this page to keep daily track of the single most important habit to emphasize this month.
Examples: taking your prenatal vitamin, drinking enough water, or doing Kegels.

month: _____

healthy habit: _____

1	2	3	4	5	6	7
8	9	10	11	12	13	14
15	16	17	18	19	20	21
22	23	24	25	26	27	28
29	30	31				

monthly health tracker

Use this page to keep daily track of the single most important habit to emphasize this month.
Examples: taking your prenatal vitamin, drinking enough water, or doing Kegels.

month: _____

healthy habit: _____

1	2	3	4	5	6	7
8	9	10	11	12	13	14
15	16	17	18	19	20	21
22	23	24	25	26	27	28
29	30	31				

monthly health tracker

Use this page to keep daily track of the single most important habit to emphasize this month. Examples: taking your prenatal vitamin, drinking enough water, or doing Kegels.

month: _____

healthy habit: _____

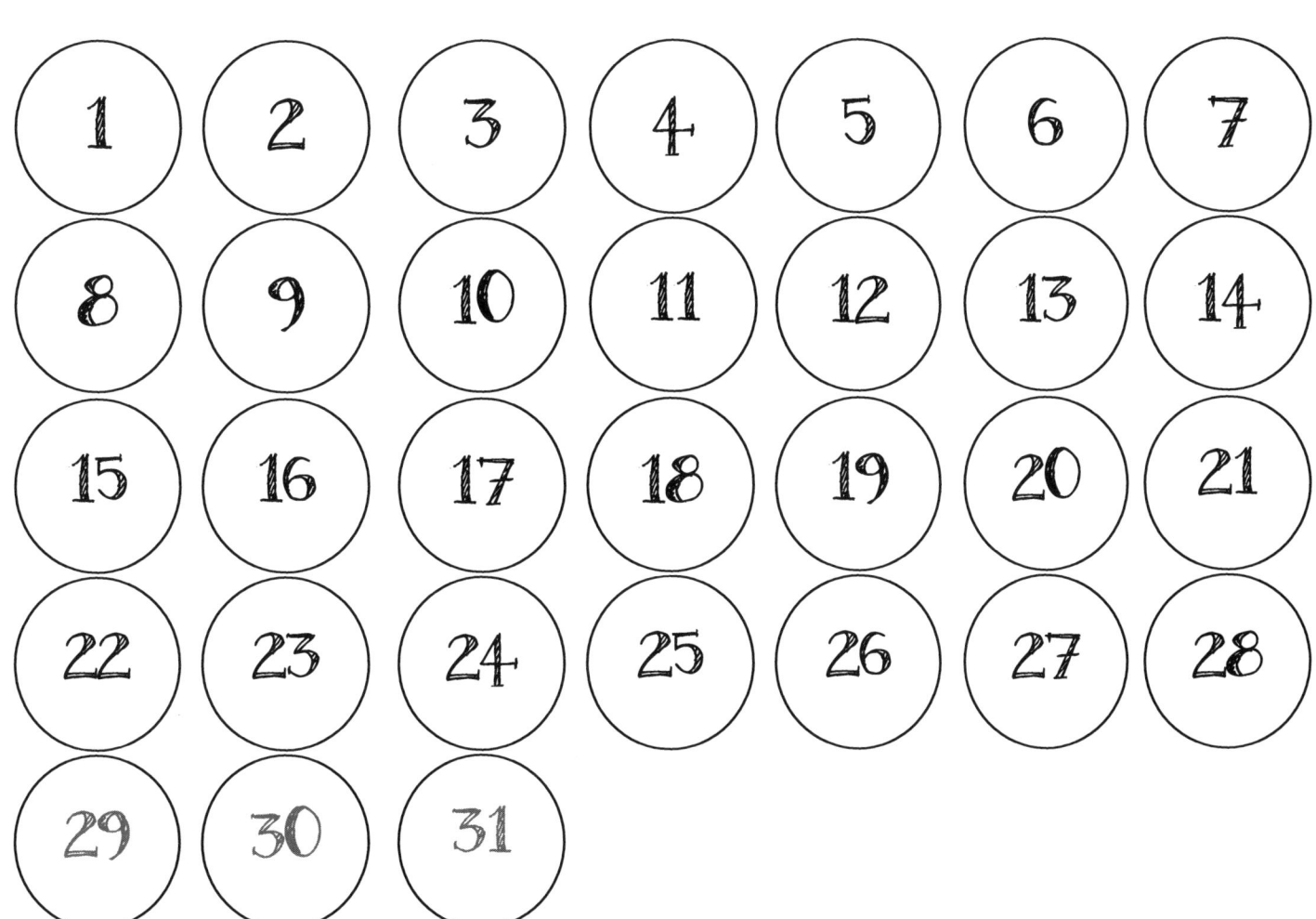

1 2 3 4 5 6 7
8 9 10 11 12 13 14
15 16 17 18 19 20 21
22 23 24 25 26 27 28
29 30 31

second trimester

weeks 14-28

basking in the glow

cross off the weeks
as you go...

14 15 16 17
18 19 20 21
22 23 24 25
26 27 28

self care

Fill in the circles as you complete each action. Feel free to use the suggested actions, or write in your own.

take a bath

prenatal yoga

take a nap

drink water

talk to a friend

_____

_____

_____

_____

_____

○ ○ ○ ○ ○ ○
○ ○ ○ ○ ○ ○
○ ○ ○ ○ ○ ○
○ ○ ○ ○ ○ ○
○ ○ ○ ○ ○ ○
○ ○ ○ ○ ○ ○

○ ○ ○ ○ ○ ○

○ ○ ○ ○ ○ ○

○ ○ ○ ○ ○ ○

○ ○ ○ ○ ○ ○

monthly health tracker

Use this page to keep daily track of the single most important habit to emphasize this month. Examples: taking your prenatal vitamin, drinking enough water, or doing Kegels.

month: _____

healthy habit: _____

1	2	3	4	5	6	7
8	9	10	11	12	13	14
15	16	17	18	19	20	21
22	23	24	25	26	27	28
29	30	31				

monthly health tracker

Use this page to keep daily track of the single most
important habit to emphasize this month.
Examples: taking your prenatal vitamin, drinking
enough water, or doing Kegels.

month: _____

healthy habit: _____

1	2	3	4	5	6	7
8	9	10	11	12	13	14
15	16	17	18	19	20	21
22	23	24	25	26	27	28
29	30	31				

monthly health tracker

Use this page to keep daily track of the single most important habit to emphasize this month. Examples: taking your prenatal vitamin, drinking enough water, or doing Kegels.

month: _____

healthy habit: _____

1	2	3	4	5	6	7
8	9	10	11	12	13	14
15	16	17	18	19	20	21
22	23	24	25	26	27	28
29	30	31				

third trimester

weeks 29-40

growing and becoming

cross off the weeks
as you go...

29 30 31 32

33 34 35 36

37 38 39 40

41 42

self care

Fill in the circles as you complete each action. Feel free to use the suggested actions, or write in your own.

take a bath

prenatal yoga

take a nap

drink water

talk to a friend

_____

_____

_____

_____

_____

monthly health tracker

Use this page to keep daily track of the single most
important habit to emphasize this month.
Examples: taking your prenatal vitamin, drinking
enough water, or doing Kegels.

month: _____

healthy habit: _____

1	2	3	4	5	6	7
8	9	10	11	12	13	14
15	16	17	18	19	20	21
22	23	24	25	26	27	28
29	30	31				

monthly health tracker

Use this page to keep daily track of the single most important habit to emphasize this month. Examples: taking your prenatal vitamin, drinking enough water, or doing Kegels.

month: _____

healthy habit: _____

1	2	3	4	5	6	7
8	9	10	11	12	13	14
15	16	17	18	19	20	21
22	23	24	25	26	27	28
29	30	31				

monthly health tracker

Use this page to keep daily track of the single most important habit to emphasize this month.
Examples: taking your prenatal vitamin, drinking enough water, or doing Kegels.

month: _____

healthy habit: _____

1	2	3	4	5	6	7
8	9	10	11	12	13	14
15	16	17	18	19	20	21
22	23	24	25	26	27	28
29	30	31				

labor & delivery

What information, strategies, and procedures do you wish to remember for when the time comes?

_____

_____

_____

_____

_____

_____

_____

my birth plan

Fill this page out with your OB, doula, and/or partner.
This format is adapted from the planning matrix found here:
http://www.birthingnaturally.net/birthplan/sample/sample1.html

Environment for labor

_____

_____

_____

Pain Management

_____

_____

_____

_____

my birth plan
page 2

In case of emergency

_____

_____

_____

Newborn care

_____

_____

_____

_____

fourth trimester

months 1-3

the birth

Describe your birth experience. How did you feel before, during, and afterwards?

_____

_____

_____

_____

_____

_____

_____

_____

_____

_____

life at home
since the birth...

_____

_____

_____

_____

_____

_____

_____

_____

monthly health tracker

Use this page to keep daily track of the single most important habit to emphasize this month. Examples: taking your prenatal vitamin, drinking enough water, or doing Kegels.

month: _____

healthy habit: _____

1 2 3 4 5 6 7

8 9 10 11 12 13 14

15 16 17 18 19 20 21

22 23 24 25 26 27 28

29 30 31

monthly health tracker

Use this page to keep daily track of the single most important habit to emphasize this month. Examples: taking your prenatal vitamin, drinking enough water, or doing Kegels.

month: _____

healthy habit: _____

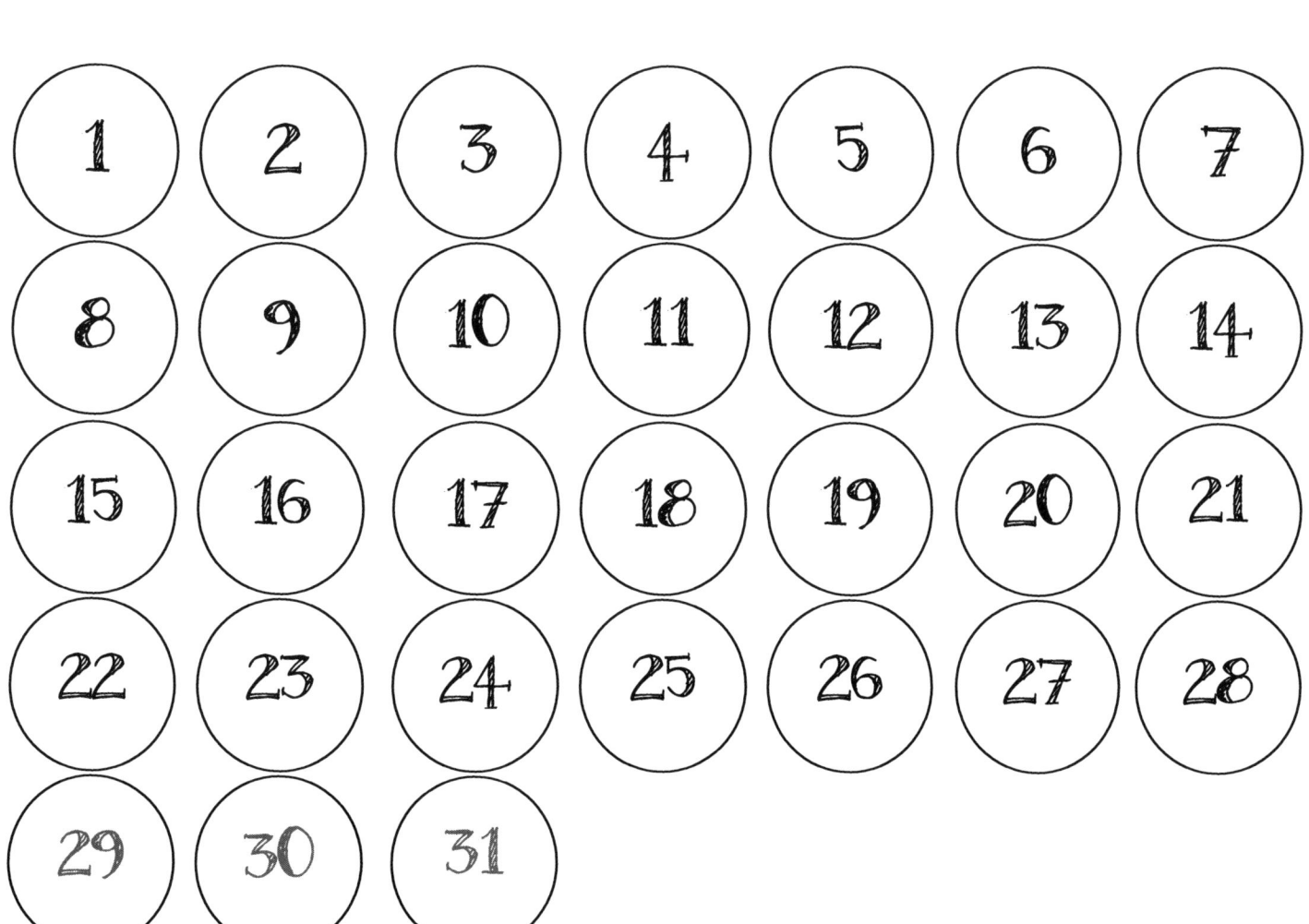

monthly health tracker

Use this page to keep daily track of the single most important habit to emphasize this month. Examples: taking your prenatal vitamin, drinking enough water, or doing Kegels.

month: _____

healthy habit: _____

how do you feel?

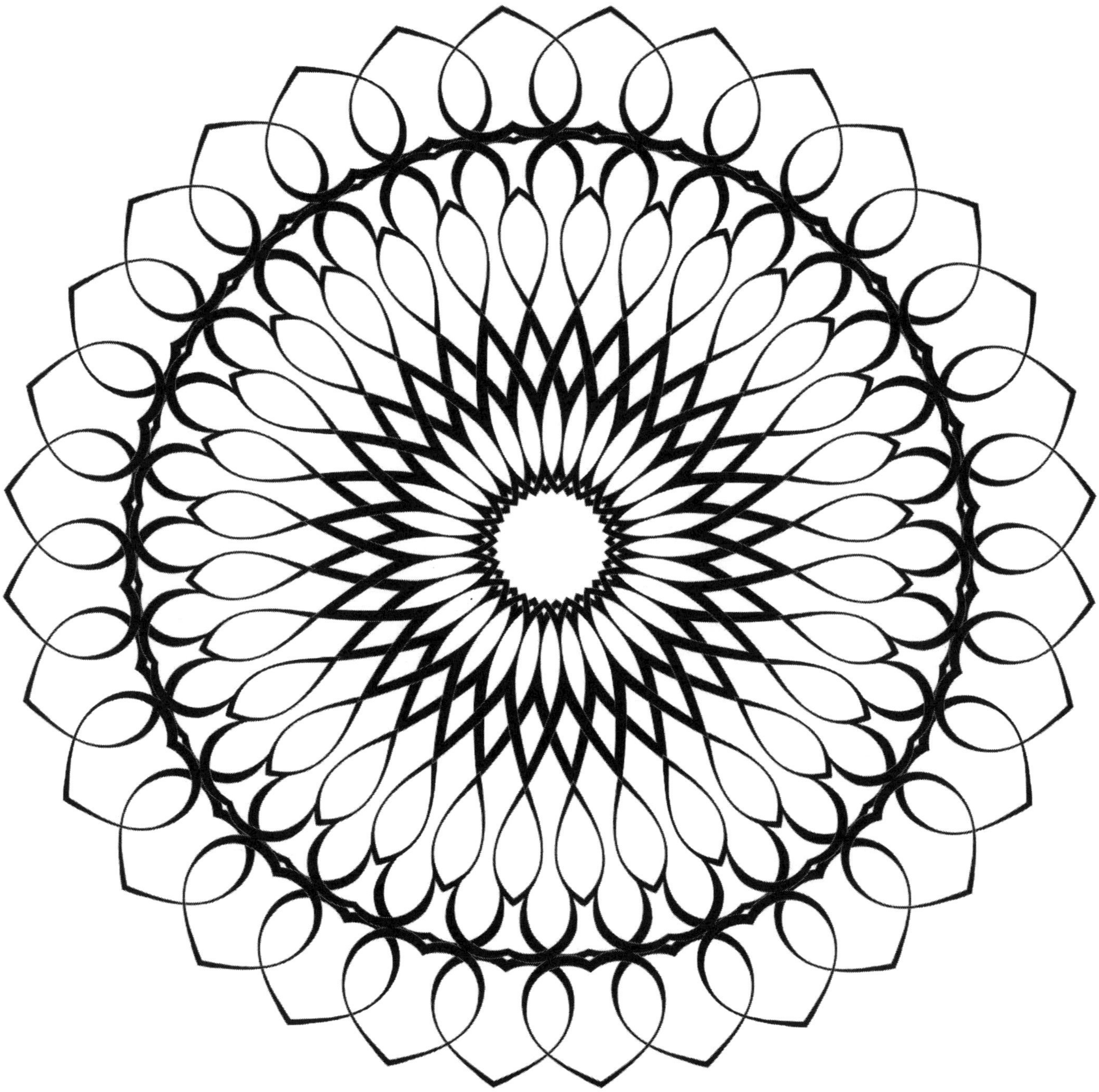

(mentally, physically, emotionally)

suggested topics
for free writing

- the first time you heard the baby's heartbeat
- the first time you felt the baby kick
- what you're doing to prepare your home and living space for the baby
- questions you'd like to ask your baby
- how your partner and family are handling your pregnancy
- funny, touching, or silly comments that have been made to you during your pregnancy
- what you're most excited, worried, or otherwise emotional about as you proceed through pregnancy
- memories from your childhood
- hopes and dreams for your baby
- hopes and dreams for yourself as you become a mother

thoughts

thoughts and feelings

_____

_____

_____

_____

_____

_____

_____

_____

_____

notes to myself

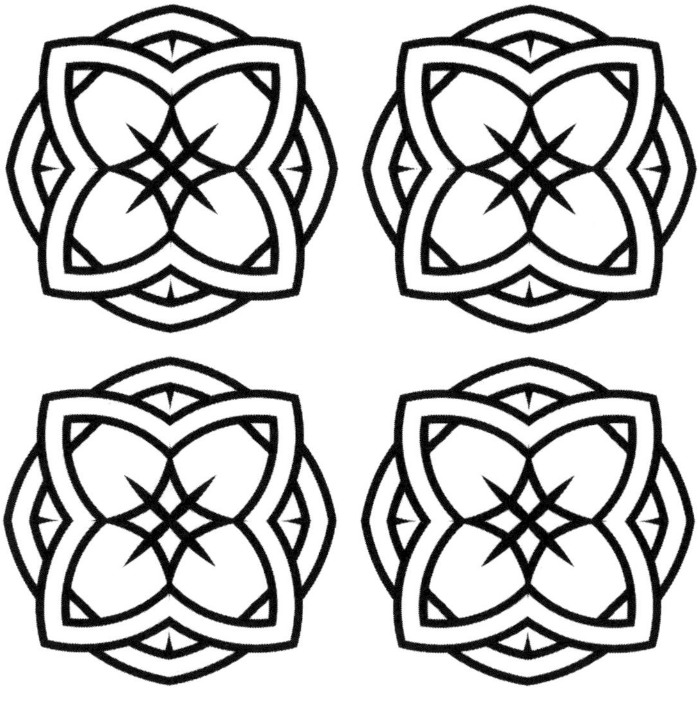

_____

_____

_____

_____

_____

_____

_____

_____

thoughts

_____

_____

_____

_____

_____

_____

_____

_____

_____

_____

_____

_____

thoughts

_____

_____

_____

_____

_____

_____

_____

_____

_____

_____

notes to myself

pregnancy
challenges

_____

_____

_____

_____

_____

_____

_____

_____

hopes & dreams

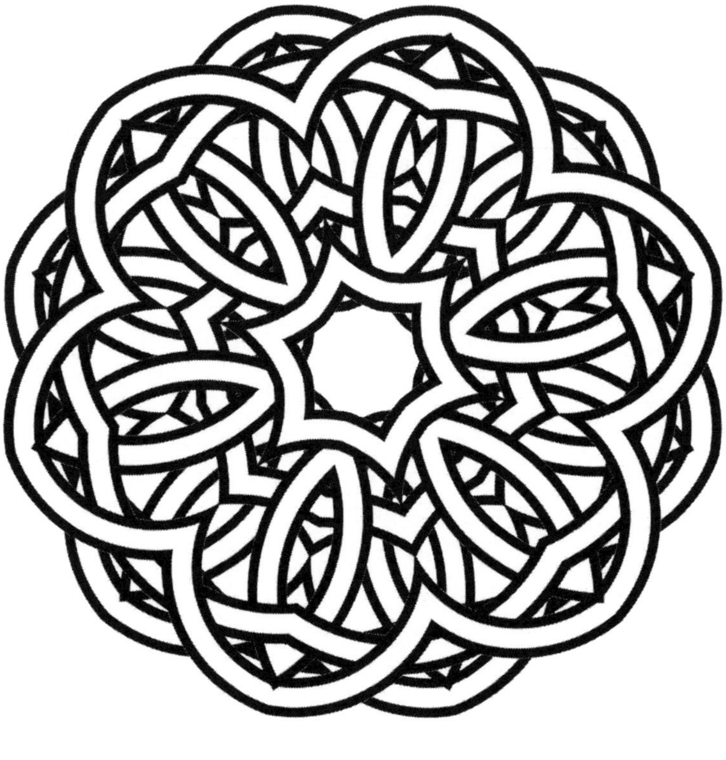

notes to myself

- -

- - - - - - - - - - - - -

- - - - - - - - - - - - -

- - - - - - - - - - - - -

- - - - - - - - - - - - -

- -

- -

- -

thoughts and feelings

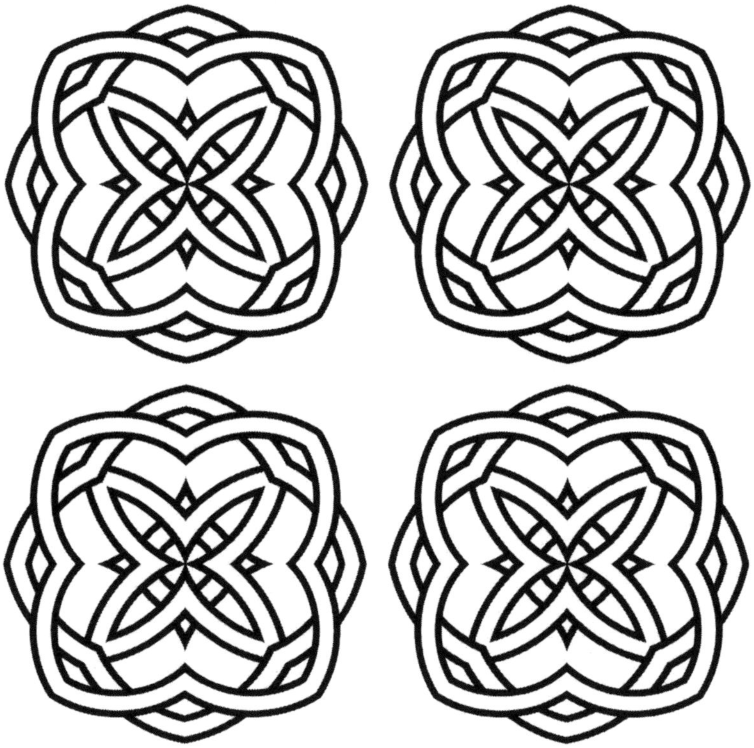

thoughts

_____

_____

_____

_____

_____

_____

_____

_____

_____

_____

_____

_____

_____

notes to myself

----

thoughts and feelings

letters to my baby

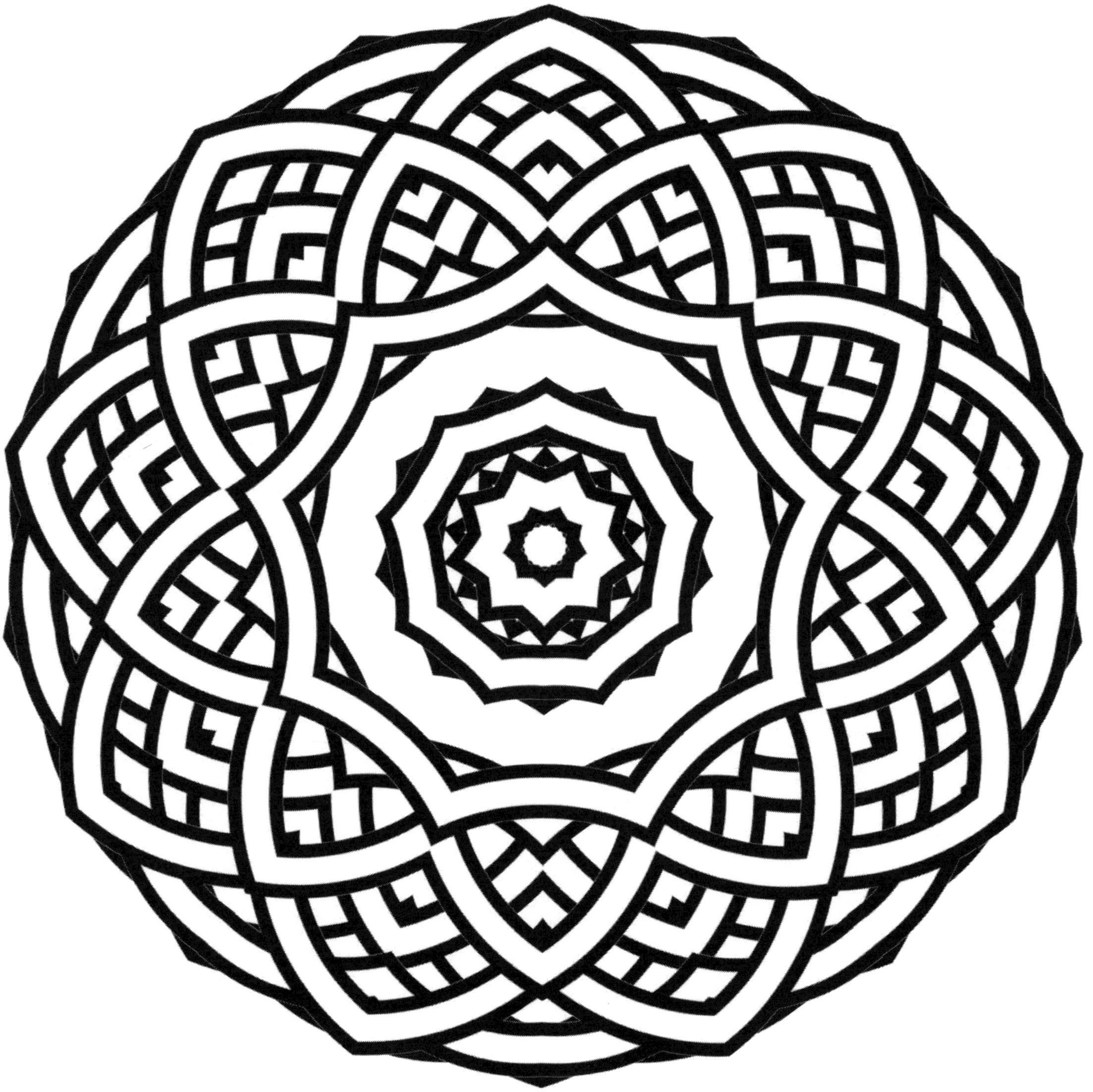

sentence starters for journaling or letter writing

If I had unlimited time and money...

What is most bothering me is...

I really want to remember...

I'd almost rather forget...

I spend a lot of time thinking about...

People don't understand that...

I love it when...

I worry when...

Here's what makes it all worthwhile...

dear baby,

_____

_____

_____

_____

_____

_____

_____

_____

_____

love, mama

dear baby,

_____

_____

_____

_____

_____

_____

_____

_____

_____

love, mama

dear baby,

_____

_____

_____

_____

_____

_____

_____

_____

_____

_____

_____

love, mama

dear baby,

_____

_____

_____

_____

_____

_____

_____

_____

_____

love, mama

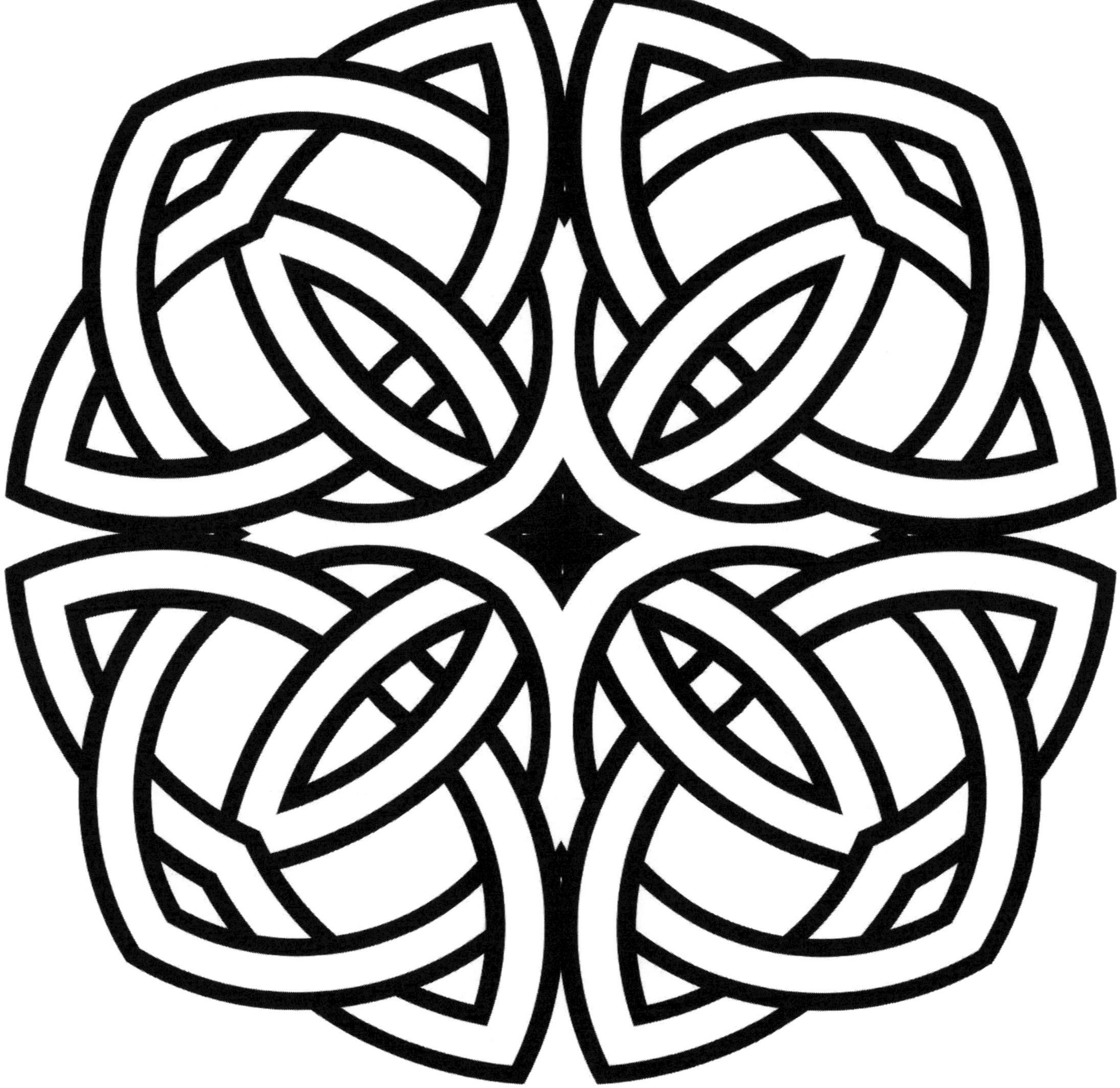

everything good
takes time

i am

becoming

my love

is strong

i am

enough

hopes &

dreams

in my own time

I am growing

love & kisses

and sleep

I am loved

and supported

thank you for choosing to spend your precious time with my designs. best of luck to you and your baby!

for more coloring books and journals, check out http:// www.turtlemoonpress.com

♡ scrap page ♡

test out your tools here!

this book is dedicated to my mom,
sharon fischler - the mother i
aspire to be

29015446R00099

Printed in Great Britain
by Amazon